Spotlight on
Japan

Bobbie Kalman
Crabtree Publishing Company
www.crabtreebooks.com

Spotlight On My Country

Author and Editor-in-Chief
Bobbie Kalman

Editor
Kathy Middleton

Proofreader
Crystal Sikkens

Fact editor
Marcella Haanstra

Photo research
Bobbie Kalman

Design
Bobbie Kalman
Katherine Berti

Print and production coordinator
Katherine Berti

Created by Bobbie Kalman

For Crystal Sikkens,
with much appreciation for everything you do

Prepress technician
Katherine Berti

Illustrations
Katherine Berti: pages 4 (map), 5 (map)
Brenda Clark: page 16
Robert MacGregor: page 6 (map)
Bonna Rouse: page 7
Margaret Amy Salter: page 6 (fish and crab)

Photographs
Photos.com: back cover, pages 13 (top), 20 (bottom right), 23 (middle right and bottom right), 28 (top left), 29 (top left and top right)
Wikimedia Commons: Chris 73: page 27 (bottom right); Kasuga: page 29 (bottom middle)
Front cover and other images by Shutterstock

Library and Archives Canada Cataloguing in Publication

Kalman, Bobbie, 1947-
     Spotlight on Japan / Bobbie Kalman.

(Spotlight on my country)
Includes index.
Issued also in an electronic format.
ISBN 978-0-7787-3459-8 (bound).--ISBN 978-0-7787-3485-7 (pbk.)

     1. Japan--Juvenile literature. I. Title. II. Series: Spotlight on my country

DS806.K355 2011   j952   C2010-905111-4

Library of Congress Cataloging-in-Publication Data

Kalman, Bobbie.
 Spotlight on Japan / Bobbie Kalman.
   p. cm. -- (Spotlight on my country)
 Includes index.
 ISBN 978-0-7787-3485-7 (pbk. : alk. paper) -- ISBN 978-0-7787-3459-8
(reinforced library binding : alk. paper) -- ISBN 978-1-4271-9538-8
(electronic PDF)
 1. Japan--Juvenile literature. I. Title. II. Series.

 DS806.K335 2011
 952--dc22

                                                                    2010027849

Crabtree Publishing Company
www.crabtreebooks.com   1-800-387-7650

Printed in the U.S.A./082010/BA20100709

Published in Canada
Crabtree Publishing
616 Welland Ave.
St. Catharines, Ontario
L2M 5V6

Published in the United States
Crabtree Publishing
PMB 59051
350 Fifth Avenue, 59th Floor
New York, New York 10118

Published in the United Kingdom
Crabtree Publishing
Maritime House
Basin Road North, Hove
BN41 1WR

Published in Australia
Crabtree Publishing
386 Mt. Alexander Rd.
Ascot Vale (Melbourne)
VIC 3032

Contents

Welcome to Japan!

Japan is a **country** that is made up of 6,852 **islands**. A country is an area of land with borders. An island is land that has water all around it. Japan's four largest islands are called Honshu, Shikoku, Kyushu, and Hokkaido. Tokyo, Japan's capital city, is on Honshu, the biggest island. The Japanese call their country *Nippon*. This Japanese word means "Land of the rising sun." Japan is in the eastern part of the world, where the sun rises.

CHINA

RUSSIA

HOKKAIDO
• Sapporo

NORTH
KOREA

Akita •

SEA OF JAPAN

*PACIFIC
OCEAN*

SOUTH
KOREA

HONSHU

**MAP OF
JAPAN**

• Tokyo
Kyoto • Nagoya *MOUNT* •Yokohama
Hiroshima *FUJI*
• • Osaka

N

W ← → E

KYUSHU SHIKOKU

Nagasaki • ▲ *MOUNT
ASO*

S

*EAST
CHINA
SEA*

▲ *MOUNT
SAKURAJIMA*
Kagoshima •

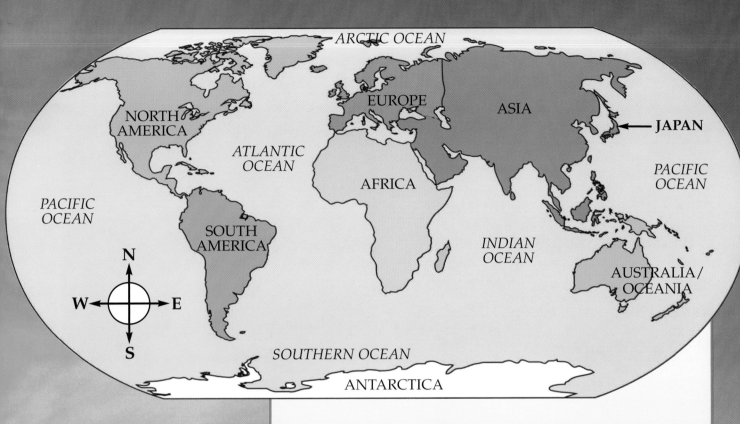

ARCTIC OCEAN

EUROPE

ASIA

→ **JAPAN**

NORTH
AMERICA

ATLANTIC
OCEAN

PACIFIC
OCEAN

AFRICA

PACIFIC
OCEAN

SOUTH
AMERICA

INDIAN
OCEAN

N

AUSTRALIA/
OCEANIA

W   E

S

SOUTHERN OCEAN

ANTARCTICA

Where is Japan?

Japan is part of the **continent** of Asia. A continent is a huge area of land. The other continents are Africa, North America, South America, Europe, Australia/Oceania, and Antarctica. The seven continents are shown on the map above. What are the names of Earth's five oceans?

Oceans and seas

The thousands of islands that make up Japan form an **archipelago**. An archipelago is a chain of islands in an ocean or sea. The Japanese Archipelago lies in the Pacific Ocean. The Sea of Japan separates Japan from Russia, North Korea, and South Korea. The East China Sea is to the south. The Sea of Okhotsk is to the north of Japan.

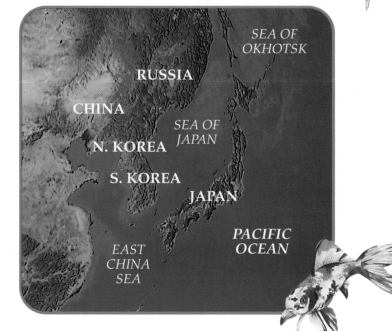

A sea is a part of an ocean that is close to land. The seas near Japan are part of the Pacific Ocean.

These small islands are near Tokyo. Some of Japan's islands are just big rocks in the ocean.

*You are never far from a beach when you are in Japan. The widest part of Japan is only 186 miles (300 km), with seashores on both sides. These girls are having a fun day **snorkeling** in the ocean.*

*Close to the islands of Japan are **coral reefs**. Coral reefs are ocean habitats with many kinds of fish and other animals. The humphead wrasse on the left lives in coral reefs in the Pacific Ocean near Japan. Olive ridley turtles also live in the ocean around Japan.*

Japan's land

Mountains cover almost four-fifths of Japan's land. On the flat lands at the bottom of mountains are cities, farms, parks, and businesses. Most of the people who live in Japan are crowded into these flat areas of land. They live in busy cities, especially in Tokyo, shown left.

*(below) Miyama is a village near the city of Kyoto, on the island of Honshu. Rice **paddies** surround this village. The houses in Miyama look like the houses in which the Japanese lived more than a thousand years ago. The forest behind the town is an old-growth forest that has never been cut down.*

*Rice is a **staple food** in Japan. A staple food is eaten every day. Today, most rice planting is done by machine, but there are still farms where planting is done by hand.*

*There are many **hot springs** in Japan that are heated by **volcanoes** (see pages 10-11). Japanese macaque monkeys, also called snow monkeys, live in the mountainous areas of Honshu, where it is very cold in winter. They spend much of their time keeping warm in the hot springs of that area.*

Volcanoes in Japan

Japan's many mountains were formed by volcanoes. A volcano is an opening in Earth's **crust**, or outer layer. Hot **magma**, ash, rocks, and gases escape from below the earth through volcanoes. More than half of Earth's volcanoes are in the Pacific Ocean in an area called the "Ring of Fire." Japan is in this area. Volcanoes can make tall mountains. Mount Fuji is the highest mountain in Japan. Some people call it an **active** volcano, and some say it is **dormant**. There are more than 80 active volcanoes in Japan.

An active volcano is one that has erupted recently or one that might erupt at any time. A dormant volcano is one that has not erupted in hundreds of years but shows signs that it might become active again. Mount Fuji last erupted in 1707–08. Do you think it is an active volcano or a dormant one?

Sakurajima and Aso

Mount Aso (right) is the biggest active volcano in Japan and is among the largest in the world. It also has one of the largest **calderas**. Sakurajima (below) is an active volcano that has been erupting since 1955. Several hundred small explosions happen each year, throwing ash high above the mountain.

*A caldera is a big circular hole that forms after a volcano erupts and **collapses**, or falls inward. Calderas often fill with rainwater. Mount Aso is on the island of Kyushu.*

Winds brought ash to nearby Kagoshima City during an eruption of Sakurajima in 2010. People wore masks to keep from breathing in the ash and gases.

Japan's early history

The first known **indigenous**, or native, people to live in Japan were the Ainu. They did not look like the Japanese people of today. Most Japanese people are the **descendants** of Chinese and Korean people who moved to Japan long ago. These people brought their languages and ways of life with them.

About 25,000 Ainu live on the island of Hokkaido, in the northern part of Japan.

samurai *warrior*

Powerful families

A long time ago, powerful families called **clans** ruled Japan. They fought one another for land and power until the leader of one of the clans became emperor. In 1192, a man named Minamoto Yorimoto took control of all the clans. He was called the *shogun*, or emperor's general. Soldiers called *samurai* defended the land controlled by the *shogun's* clans.

This picture shows the celebration of Minamoto Yorimoto becoming shogun *of Japan.*

Festival of Ages

The Festival of Ages, or *Jidai Matsuri,* is held in Kyoto each year to remember Japan's early history. People dress in costumes from the past and march through the streets. They dress as *samurai,* farmers, and *shoguns.* Many women wear colorful *kimonos.*

kimono

Past and present

The national flag of Japan is white with a large red circle in the center that stands for the sun.

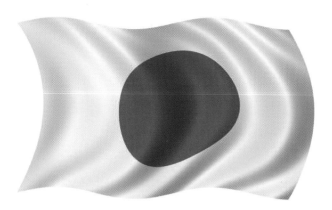

The Japanese emperor lives in the Imperial Palace in Tokyo.

The Japanese Diet works in this building, which is also in Tokyo.

For 700 years, Japan was ruled by *shoguns* and their *samurai*. During that time, Japanese people were not allowed to leave Japan, and people from other places were not allowed to enter the country.

Americans in Japan

In 1853, an American naval officer named Commodore Perry sailed to Japan to set up trade. A few years later, Emperor Meiji took over rule from the *shogun* and opened Japan to the world.

Japan is a democracy

Today, Japan still has an emperor, but the country is a **democracy**. In a democracy, people **elect**, or vote for, their leaders. The head of Japan's government is a prime minister, and the elected government representatives make up the Diet, or parliament.

In 1945, near the end of World War II, the United States dropped two **atomic** bombs on Japan—one on Nagasaki, the other on Hiroshima. The bombs killed more than 200,000 people. The ruins of the only building left standing in the area where the first bomb dropped became a monument called the Hiroshima Peace Memorial. It reminds people of how terrible war is! The story on the following pages is about a girl who lived in Hiroshima when the bomb fell.

15

Sadako's story

A young girl named Sadako Sasaki was two years old when the bomb was dropped on Hiroshima, her city. Ten years later, Sadako became ill with **leukemia**, a type of cancer. While she was in the hospital, she made paper cranes using the Japanese paper-folding art of *origami* (see page 28). She believed that if she could fold 1,000 cranes, her wishes would come true. She wished to grow old and to have peace on Earth.

Everyone who visited Sadako brought *origami* paper for her cranes. Sadako kept folding cranes until she died in 1955.

Sadako's monument to peace

After Sadako died, many children folded cranes to share in Sadako's wish for peace. This monument was built to remember Sadako. Children visit the monument and leave paper cranes to add their wishes for world peace.

Japan's cities

Japan's biggest cities are Tokyo, Osaka, Yokohama, and Nagoya. They are crowded along the coast of Honshu island. More than twelve million people live in Tokyo, Japan's capital city. Kyoto is a city that shows life in old Japan. It has beautiful parks, teahouses, and more than 2,000 temples and **shrines**.

Tokyo is a big city with tall office buildings, shops, and theaters. It also has beautiful parks.

(left) The Umeda Sky Building in Osaka is made up of two 40-story towers that are joined at their top stories. Wide skywalks at the center allow people to walk from one building to another.

(above) Yokohama is Japan's second-biggest city. Its Minato Mirai area has a large ferris wheel and tall buildings.

Kyoto is known for its gardens, castles, and temples. This Buddhist temple is called the Golden Pavilion. It is covered in real gold.

The people of Japan

Although Japanese people work at modern jobs and lead very modern lives, traditions from the past are also very important to them. Parents teach their children to be loyal, responsible, and well behaved. Older family members are respected and valued for their wisdom. Grandparents teach their grandchildren Japanese customs and traditions. They are important family members who often live with their children and grandchildren.

Elderly family members are treated with respect.

It is fun to spend a day with Grandmother!

20

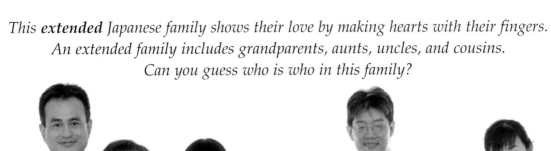

This **extended** Japanese family shows their love by making hearts with their fingers.
An extended family includes grandparents, aunts, uncles, and cousins.
Can you guess who is who in this family?

Getting a good education is very
important to the Japanese. These
students attend a university
in Tokyo.

Celebrating children

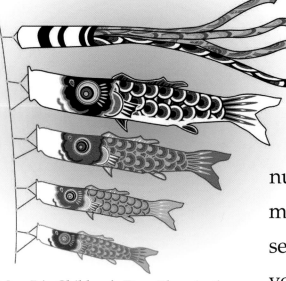

May 5 is Children's Day. Flags in the shape of **carp***, a symbol of strength, are flown to remind children to be strong and to face their challenges.*

Japanese children have many special days to celebrate. The numbers three, five, and seven are a big part of these celebrations. People believe these numbers are lucky. For example, which months in the year are the third, fifth, and seventh? What number do you get when you add the three lucky numbers together? Which children's day in Japan contains this number? Read the next page to find out!

The Hina Matsuri, *or Doll Festival, is on March 3. Girls dress in their best* kimonos *and display their family dolls on that day.* (See page 29.)

Shichi-go-san

Shichi-go-san means seven-five-three in Japanese. On November 15, children of these ages dress in **traditional** clothes, go to a shrine to pray, and receive many presents at parties with family and friends. This day is like a big birthday party.

Dolls are an important part of many celebrations. Families collect dolls that show Japan's history.

Name four ways that this girl and her doll look alike.

23

Two religions

Japan's two main religions are Shinto and Buddhism. They both play important roles in celebrations and in the Japanese way of life. Shinto teaches people to respect nature and to remember the heroes from the past. It is a way of looking at family life, art, and sports, as well as spiritual life. Those who practice Shinto believe that gods and goddesses live in the water, animals, plants, and in the sun. These *kami*, or spirits, protect people. Amaterasu, the sun goddess, is the most important *kami*. People believe that all of Japan's emperors are descended from her.

People dressed in costumes from the past are carrying a portable shrine from the old Imperial Palace to the Heian Shinto shrine in Kyoto as part of the Festival of Ages. The portable shrines represent the spirit of two emperors—Kammu and Komei.

Buddhism in Japan

Buddhism came to Japan from China and Korea. The Japanese practice different kinds of Buddhism. There are many big Buddhas carved into cliffs and mountains in Japan. This giant Buddha is a Buddha of Medicine and Healing. It is 101 feet (31 m) high. It holds a medicine jar.

Japanese culture

Culture is the way people live. It is the food they eat, the music they enjoy, the clothes they wear, the art they create, and the ways they celebrate. Most Japanese people have the same culture. They share the same values and beliefs, and they celebrate in the same ways. They live between two worlds. One is their modern way of life, and the other is their respect for the old traditions passed down to them from their ancestors.

This picture shows the old and new cultures of Japan. These two women, dressed in kimonos from the past, are standing outside a Buddhist temple. They are looking at the tall buildings of the city below them.

These young girls are performing a dance to celebrate the start of the autumn season.

Karate is a martial art that teaches self-defense. It also teaches respect.

Drumming is part of most Japanese celebrations. Taiko means "drum" in Japanese. Above, the giant taiko drum was made out of a single piece of wood from a 1200-year-old tree. It weighs about three tons (2.7 metric tons).

Old and new art

The Japanese have developed special kinds of art that show their history and culture. They have also created some new forms of cartoon art, called *manga* and *anime*, which young people all over the world are enjoying and copying. These pages show some of Japan's old and new art forms.

*The plate on the right shows the Japanese art of **story painting**. It tells a story of the Japanese way of life.*

*The lantern above is painted with a Japanese **caricature**. A caricature is a cartoon painting of a person.*

Origami is a way of folding paper into many kinds of objects without cutting or pasting. Sadako folded hundreds of paper cranes using origami. The giraffe, elephant, and kangaroo on the left are more examples of origami art.

Dolls, dolls, dolls!

In Japan, dolls are works of art. They are displayed during many celebrations and are passed down to family members. The doll on the left is a *kokeshi* doll. *Kokeshi* dolls are made of wood. They have large shiny heads and slender bodies. *Hina* dolls are part of *Hina Matsuri*, the doll festival. They can be made of many materials. The traditional *hina* doll has a carved wooden head and hands and human or silk hair.

hina *doll*

kokeshi *doll*

Manga and anime

Manga is Japanese comic-book art. *Anime* is *manga*-style animated cartoons. Young people, such as the girl on the right, sometimes dress up to look like their favorite *manga* and *anime* characters. The characters have big eyes and wear fun clothes.

Japanese food

Not only is Japanese food delicious, it looks beautiful, too. People buy their fruits, vegetables, and meat fresh at a market each day. Rice is used to make cookies, cakes, crackers, and noodles. Rice noodles are a favorite food. They are served with fish or meat broth and chopped vegetables.

These children are eating noodle soup, salad, fish, meat, and rice. The girl is eating with chopsticks. Her brother is eating with his fingers. He is learning to use chopsticks.

The food above looks like a work of art. It tastes wonderful, too!

Meals are often served in bento boxes. Bento boxes are made of wood or shiny black plastic. The boxes are divided into sections, each containing a different kind of food. This box contains rice, salad, shrimp, and meat.

This delicious dessert is made with fresh fruits and chocolate. YUM!

This boat is filled with sushi. Sushi is rolls or balls of sticky rice with seafood or vegetables inside or on top. The caterpillar above is also made of sushi.

31

Glossary

Note: Some boldfaced words are defined where they appear in the book.

active Describing a volcano that has erupted recently or may soon erupt

anime Japanese animation using *manga*-style cartoon art

archipelago A chain of islands

atomic Something that is highly explosive and leaves radiation, often causing illness

carp Strong fish that can swim upstream and jump high out of the water

coral reef An ocean area made up of living coral animals and skeletons of dead corals

democracy A form of government that has been chosen by the people of a country

descendant A person who is related to someone who lived long ago

extended Referring to family members that include more than just parents and their children

hot spring A warm-water spring that is heated by volcanoes inside the earth

indigenous Describing people who are the first to live in a particular area

kimono A loose fitting robe that is tied with a wide belt and which has big sleeves

magma Hot liquid rock deep inside Earth

manga A Japanese comic-book art style

paddy A flooded rice field

shrine A place of worship

snorkeling Swimming underwater using a mask and snorkel

traditional Referring to customs and traditions from long ago

Index